BEYONCÉ

Publisher and Creative Director: Nick Wells
Project Editor: Polly Prior
Picture Research: Emma Chafer and Polly Prior
Art Director: Mike Spender
Layout Design: Jane Ashley
Digital Design and Production: Chris Herbert

Special thanks to: Emma Chafer, Esme Chapman and Daniela Nava

FLAME TREE PUBLISHING
Crabtree Hall, Crabtree Lane
Fulham, London SW6 6TY
United Kingdom
www.flametreepublishing.com

Website for this book: www.flametreepop.com

First published 2013

13 15 17 16 14
1 3 5 7 9 10 8 6 4 2

© 2013 Flame Tree Publishing Ltd

A CIP record for this book is available from the British Library upon request.

ISBN 978-0-85775-867-5

Printed in China

BEYONCÉ

UNOFFICIAL

Caroline Corcoran
Foreword by Malcolm Mackenzie

**FLAME TREE
PUBLISHING**

Contents

Foreword

5

Something About The Girl

6

Me, Myself And I

17

In Full Flight

34

Further Information

48

Biographies & Picture Credits

48

Foreword

Beyoncé's greatest asset – aside from her voice, her moves, her songwriting abilities, her business mind and the way she fits into her Deréon jeans – is her commitment. She is focused like no other pop star, putting 100 per cent of herself into everything she does. See her incredible live shows and you'll never doubt it.

Now watch the video for 'Single Ladies (Put A Ring On It)'. Who learns impossible dance routines these days? No one. Most celebrities can't be bothered. Not Beyoncé. She sees the end game. It's not about paying the leccy bill, or even having a quickie hit, it's about the legacy. She's in it for the long haul, but frankly Mrs Carter, you are already a legend.

Kanye West may be a buffoon, but he wasn't wrong when he stormed the 2009 MTV Awards in horror when Taylor Swift's video won over Beyoncé's groundbreaking 'Single Ladies' clip that's easily the most iconic pop video since Kylie's 'Can't Get You Out Of My Head' and '…Baby One More Time' by Britney.

Some of us mortals are slightly mistrustful of Beyoncé. Surely she's too perfect? How can a woman be this beautiful and this smart and this talented? She was amazing in Destiny's Child, she's an equally amazing solo artist, she's a flipping good actress: heck I even loved her rapping in MTV's hip-hopera *Carmen*. But B does have one weakness… a love of fabrics best suited to DFS than DKNY. But never mind that.

Who runs the world? Have you not been paying attention? She does!

Malcolm Mackenzie
Editor, We Love Pop

Something About The Girl

Introducing Mrs Beyoncé Knowles-Carter: owner of 17 Grammys (six of them won in one night), one half of the world's only billionaire celebrity couple, 12 MTV Video Music Awards, seven Billboard Music Awards and four American Music Awards. The world might not have a clue what goes on inside her home, but one thing it does know is that on her shelves there are a lot of awards.

Being Bey

Beyoncé's music knows no age limit and she is adored by all of her fans who appreciate the sort of role model she has become to young girls. Although the singer tries to keep her private life away from the spotlight, the media are always hungry for any little detail. However, you won't find embarrassing pictures of her plastered all over the front pages every day: her behaviour is impeccable.

'It makes you feel more than alive.
Technically it's perfect, the ultimate tune
for the holy sphere of the dancefloor.'
NME on 'Crazy In Love'

'I don't like to gamble but if there's one thing I am willing to bet on it's myself.'

Beyoncé

Supremely Talented

The road to forming the group Destiny's Child was not an easy one and proved just how determined Beyoncé was to achieve success. After the initial line-up wobbles, the group found their feet, got that crucial backing from Columbia Records and sprinted off into the girl band history books.

After 'Say My Name', the hits kept coming, with 'Jumpin, Jumpin' – the final single from *The Writing's on the Wall* (1999) – and then the next album, *Survivor* (2001), which made No. 1s from every single released from it: 'Bootylicious', 'Survivor', 'Emotion' and 'Independent Women Part I'. The latter also saw Destiny's Child featuring on the movie soundtrack to *Charlie's Angels*. The album was critically received too, with music writers talking of a 'rare individuality, and a hint of genius'.

'No matter what happens, we will always love each other as friends and sisters.'

Destiny's Child after their split

Going Solo

Yes, Beyoncé was cool in Destiny's Child but when she went solo, something happened to propel her into another league. What Beyoncé was proving during the group's hiatus with 'Crazy In Love' was that she also had the stage presence to be a solo artist. 'Crazy In Love' won two Grammys, went to No. 1 in multiple countries and was critically lauded.

When the album *Dangerously In Love* (2003) was released, the hits kept coming. First of all, the dancehall-influenced 'Baby Boy' which featured Sean Paul flew to No. 1 in the *Billboard* Hot 100 and stayed there for an epic nine weeks. Then came the single 'Me, Myself and I', followed by 'Naughty Girl' – both not quite the monster hits of the first two but solid releases nonetheless; Beyoncé had just set the bar extremely high.

Dangerously In Love went to No. 1 in the US, the UK and around the world, going multi-platinum and earning Beyoncé five Grammys. If there had been any doubts, this album answered them: Beyoncé was more than up to the job of being a solo artist.

'They told me I didn't have one hit on my album. I guess they were kind of right. I had five!'

Beyoncé on Dangerously In Love

Soul Survivor

It was her twenty-fifth birthday and Destiny's Child were now officially part of Beyoncé's past – not her present, thanks to the band's 2005 split. Therefore, with the release of the commonly deemed 'difficult second album' – the sweetly titled *B'Day* (2006) – the singer wasn't just dipping a toe into solo stardom but rather diving headfirst.

B'Day was also nominated for six Grammys, with Bey walking – actually, probably strutting – away with the award for 'Best Contemporary R&B Album'. Although they had to endure a bit of a wait, Beyoncé's fans were not left disappointed by her second album. Moreover, they soon discovered that they would have the chance to see her in person, as she began the tour that would take her all around the world.

More than anything, though, *B'Day* marked the official beginning of the singer's solo career. Whatever success *Dangerously In Love* had had, at the time of its release Beyoncé was still part of the Destiny's Child entity; however, by the time *B'Day* came out, she was staking her claim to be America's next big female solo artist – and who would have bet against her?

'I think it's healthy … to be nervous. It means you care — that you … want to give a great performance.'

Beyoncé

'I feel like I'm highly respected, which is more important than any award or any amount of records.'

Beyoncé

Me, Myself and I

Beyoncé started life as a usual Texas girl, with an unusual Texan name. Beyoncé is actually a homage to her mum Tina's maiden name, Beyincé, which may provide a clue to Bey's early feminist influences. Tina didn't just refuse to let go of that name, which was about to die out; she kept hold of it and then sent it stratospheric.

As a seven-year-old, Beyoncé was entered into a talent contest, thanks to her dance teacher who spotted her potential, where she won for her performance of John Lennon's 'Imagine'. After that Bey's life took a different turn, as she focused on music at the Parker Elementary School in Houston (singing solos with the school choir) and then the High School for the Performing and Visual Arts.

Who Does She Love?

As is the case for all artists, Beyoncé has been influenced by other singers – some older ones who have recently passed away and other, more recent ones. However, despite her young age, Bey is finding that, increasingly, *she* has become the role model for girls to look up to for inspiration.

You don't become an artist like Beyoncé without having a genuine passion for music and other musicians. She spent her youth soaking up the influence of the greats – Diana Ross, Whitney Houston and Aretha Franklin.

For Beyoncé, the influences on her music are constantly changing and evolving. 'I started off being inspired by [Afrobeat music pioneer] Fela Kuti … I also found a lot of inspiration in '90s R&B, Earth, Wind & Fire, DeBarge, Lionel Richie, Teena Marie,' she said about making the album *4* (2011). 'I listened to a lot of Jackson 5 and New Edition, but also Adele, Florence + the Machine and Prince.'

'She was the ultimate legend … Her voice was perfect. Strong but soothing. Soulful and classic. Her vibrato, her cadence, her control.'

Beyoncé on Whitney Houston

Girl Crush

The irony is, of course, that many of Beyoncé's more modern influences are artists who have also been influenced *by* her. Adele has been outspoken about her girl crush on Bey, telling *Vogue* in 2013: 'I love how all of her songs are about empowerment. Even when she's married and Jay-Z put a ring on it, she releases "Single Ladies"'.

First Lady of R&B

'The first...' is the start of many sentences about Beyoncé: the first African-American woman to win the American Society of Composers, Authors and Publishers' (ASCAP) 'Songwriter of the Year' award and, in 2011, the first woman to play the main stage at Glastonbury, where reports of 'the sheer visceral power of her voice' overtook any doubts that Beyoncé's brand of fierce R&B pop might not fit on a main stage normally known for its guitar bands.

'I'm with my mother who reminds me,
"Girl, you are not a Queen."
So it's good to have some balance.'

Beyoncé

Silver Screen

A woman of many talents, Beyoncé's attempt at breaking into the world of cinema has so far returned mixed results. Knowing how determined she is, though, it's fair to say that it won't be long before she reaches the success that she deserves.

First up came Beyoncé's role in *Carmen: A Hip Hopera* in 2001 where, ironically, she played an aspiring actress. The role was followed by light-hearted parts alongside Mike Myers in *Austin Powers in Goldmember* (2002) and Cuba Gooding Jr. in *The Fighting Temptations* (2003).

The Dreamgirl

Perhaps *Dreamgirls* – the story of a female pop group in the 1960s and of a controlling, abusive manager – was the one that was most expected to give Beyoncé kudos in the acting world. And maybe it would have, if she had not been overshadowed, according to most reviewers, by a young Jennifer Hudson, who won a Best Supporting Actress Oscar for it.

In 2008's *Cadillac Records*, Beyoncé, who played Etta James, hinted at more depth to come from her acting but the praise was not forthcoming.

Onwards and Upwards

Despite being busy Beyoncé keeps plugging away within the movie world, most recently working on the soundtrack to *The Great Gatsby* with a re-recording of Amy Winehouse's 'Back to Black'.

In 2013, Beyoncé also saw the release of 3D animated movie *Epic*, where she provided the voice of Queen Tara, the ruler of the forest where teenager M. K. (Amanda Seyfried) is suddenly transported. It's a bit of a departure but one that makes sense when Beyoncé places it in the context of the arrival of children into her life.

'… If you work hard, whatever you want, it will come to you. I know that's easier said than done but keep trying.'

Beyoncé

How Does She Look?

Effortlessly beautiful – with or without makeup – Beyoncé would look good wearing anything; but her great taste means that certain items of clothing that she chose for her videos have become almost as famous as her songs.

Beyoncé admits that her music and her style go hand in hand; when she hears a single, she immediately knows the look that will go with it. It makes sense, really – who can imagine the 'Single Ladies' video without the one-shouldered bodysuit or 'Crazy In Love' without the denim hot pants and vest strutting towards us?

On The Other Side

These days, of course, Bey goes beyond wearing the clothes; she is on the other side. As well as working with H&M – she signed a deal as the face of the brand in 2013 – Beyoncé has her own clothing range, House of Deréon. However it was in 2013, that Bey really 'arrived' in fashion circles. Being invited to be the Honorary Chair of the Metropolitan Museum of Art Costume Institute Gala, hosted annually by American *Vogue* editor Anna Wintour, was a sign that Beyoncé was now being taken seriously by the fashion set.

'I only allow myself one day to feel sorry for myself.

People who complain really get on my nerves.'

Beyoncé

'I love my husband, but it is nothing like a conversation with a woman that understands you. I grow so much from those conversations.'

Beyoncé in 'Life Is But A Dream'

Family Affair

Beyoncé's family have been involved from the very beginning in her career and have always been really supportive, even becoming part of her workforce. While Beyoncé's mum Tina became her stylist, her dad Mathew, who already worked in the music business, became her manager. As is often the case, though, relationships can go wrong, and Bey has had to overcome the trauma of her parents' very public divorce.

Mathew and Beyoncé's professional relationship also ended in 2011 with Beyoncé telling *Oprah* in 2013 that they simply had 'issues' over who was in control. She opened up further about it in her 2013 documentary 'Life Is But A Dream', explaining that juggling a professional and personal life became difficult and that she needed Mathew as a father.

Beyoncé's own clothing range, House of Deréon. is run with her stylist and designer mum, Tina. It is a proper family business – where Bey's sister Solange often models – and was inspired by their grandmother, the late Agnèz Deréon.

'Love is something that never goes out of style. It's something everybody experiences … people usually want to feel that.'

Beyoncé

Perfect Match

Part of Bey's popularity *has* to lie in her marriage to Jay-Z. She made it clear that she wanted a husband who was her equal, and her fans respected her all the more for that. After their marriage in 2008, Beyoncé and Jay-Z became the ultimate music power couple.

In January 2012, Beyoncé gave birth to a daughter, Blue Ivy, after a suitably dramatic pregnancy reveal. At the 2011 Video Music Awards, Beyoncé threw her microphone on the stage floor and ripped open her blazer after a performance of 'Love On Top', saying 'I want you to feel the love that's growing inside me.' What a way to share her secret!

In Full Flight

Taking inspiration from her on-stage alter ego 'Sasha Fierce' she was back with album number three, entitled *I am … Sasha Fierce* (2008).

From the album came 'If I Were a Boy', 'Halo' and, perhaps most importantly, 'Single Ladies (Put A Ring On It)'. The latter did not just become the anthem of girls' nights out across the world but also spurned arguably the most well-known dance craze of the century – before Psy came along with 'Gangnam Style', of course.

'Her birth was emotional and extremely peaceful, we are in heaven … We are thankful to everyone for all your prayers.'

Beyoncé on Blue Ivy's birth

Labour Of Love

It was a more relaxed and mature Bey who released the album *4* and also embraced motherhood. Moreover, even though she still guarded her private life very closely, she decided to share with the public certain details of some incredibly painful times in her life: a past miscarriage and the professional split from her dad, who had been her manager since the very beginning of her musical career.

On its release, *4* headed straight to the top of the *Billboard* 200. The first single from it, 'Run the World (Girls)' was another standout female anthem. Followed by 'Best Thing I Never Had', 'Countdown' and 'Love on Top', *4* was delivering the hits.

The next thing Beyoncé chose to do was a series of intimate gigs – four of them, of course – in New York. The gigs sold out in 22 seconds and were critically praised, especially considering that these were far different circumstances from what Beyoncé was used to.

Mrs Carter vs Beyoncé

It can't be easy to find the right balance between the desire to have a private life away from the spotlight and being a public figure. Beyoncé, however, seems to have done just that: her family life is shielded from the media glare and her fans appear to respect this decision.

For years Beyoncé did not even acknowledge her relationship with the future father of her children. However, since she and Jay-Z got married in 2008 – and even more so since the pair had their daughter Blue Ivy – that side of her life has been acknowledged a lot more. In fact, in 2013 she made her biggest public acknowledgement of her husband to date by announcing the name of her new tour: the Mrs Carter Show.

'I feel like Mrs Carter is who I am, but more bold and more fearless than I've ever been.'

Beyoncé

Social Media Savvy

Meanwhile, Bey was taking small steps to reveal bits of her life to her fans by making clever choices with a website full of quality images of her family.

Instead of getting bored by relentless images, fans end up craving more, loving the authenticity of the pictures and posts, and the beautiful images of family life. Beyoncé has been praised for how she has been using social media and heralded as someone who really knows how to build a brand. In fact, social media Beyoncé has a lot in common with real life Beyoncé: classy, beautiful and only willing to reveal as much as she is comfortable with when it comes to that all-important home life.

Say It Loud

Increasingly, Beyoncé uses her fame for a greater good, championing important causes that matter to her.

'If you like it, you should be able to put a ring on it,' said Beyoncé's handwritten note, posted on Instagram with the hashtag #wewillunite4marriageequality. She had previously been vocal about her belief that preventing gay people from getting married is equivalent to racism: another form of prejudice.

Demanding A Plan

Beyoncé has always been a philanthropist and nowhere was that more evident than when she and her family, including fellow Destiny's girl Kelly Rowland, founded the Survivor Foundation: a charity that endeavours to help victims to get back on their feet after disasters. Originally launched after Hurricane Katrina, the charity has raised millions.

In 2010 Beyoncé and her mum opened the Beyoncé Cosmetology Center at the Brooklyn Phoenix House, which treats men and women with drug and alcohol addiction. The idea was to provide vocational beauty training to people at Phoenix House, where Beyoncé initially visited as part of her research for a film role.

My parents taught my sister and me the importance of giving back and making a difference in another person's life.'

Beyoncé

Two First Ladies

In 2013 Beyoncé threw her weight behind her latest initiative: Chime for Change – a global campaign for girls' and women's empowerment that's been termed 'Feminist Live Aid'. The pinnacle was a concert on 1 June which saw Beyoncé and other female heavyweights perform in London.

All of this obviously plays a key part in the close relationship that Beyoncé has with the US President and his wife, which began, really, with a simple case of mutual appreciation: Beyoncé is a great supporter of Obama and the President believes that Beyoncé is a great idol for his two young daughters.

When Beyoncé sung Etta James's 'At Last' at Obama's inauguration, it was a seminal moment. It also led to the singer performing at the President's second inauguration, where she sang the National Anthem.

'Barack's just a very special person and he was born to do what he does, and Michelle was born to do what she does.'

Beyoncé

World Takeover

Through the ups and downs of 2013, Beyoncé has emerged as a strong, confident and ever more popular superstar. What is going to happen next? We can only wait and see …

If something is having its moment now, Beyoncé is probably involved. She bagged the 2013 Grammy for Best Traditional R&B Performance (for 'Love On Top') and pride of place on the soundtrack of 2013's biggest film release: *The Great Gatsby* with her cover of Amy Winehouse's 'Back to Black'. Turn the TV on and there is a Beyoncé Pepsi advert; go shopping and she's staring at you in a bikini in H&M.

'No one has that voice, no one moves the way she moves, no one can hold an audience the way she does.'

Baz Luhrmann

A Megastar For A New Generation

Consensus from those who saw the Mrs Carter tour was that there could be no better: Bey was a superstar – a megastar for a new generation. 'She had a star wattage that was blinding, an ability to sing and dance and be mesmerizing,' said one review.

But what about the now surely overdue fifth album? Don't worry, everyone, Bey's best girl pal Gwyneth Paltrow tells us that it is definitely coming soon – and if anyone knows, it's Gwyneth. And after that? Well, we could expect anything, as Beyoncé's own words tell us: 'I'm telling my daughter every day, "You know you can be president, you know it's possible,"' she says.

Beyoncé for president? You wouldn't bet against it.

To J and B, thank you so much for your friendship. Beyoncé could not be a better role model for my girls.'

President Obama on Beyoncé and Jay-Z

Beyoncé Vital Info

Birth Name	Beyoncé Giselle Knowles
Birth Date	4 September 1981
Birth Place	Houston, Texas, US
Nationality	American
Height	1.67 m (5 ft 6 in)
Hair Colour	Golden Brown
Eye Colour	Hazel

Online

beyonce.com:	Beyoncé's official site packed with all the must-know information about the global superstar
twitter.com/Beyonce:	Join millions of others and follow @Beyonce for her very own Twitter updates
facebook.com/beyonce:	With millions of likes and thousands of photos Beyoncé's Facebook page has exclusive posts and updates
youtube.com/artist/beyoncé:	Beyoncé's official YouTube channel is packed with all the singer's music videos
flametreepop.com:	Celebrity, fashion and pop news, with loads of links, downloads and free stuff!

Acknowledgements

Caroline Corcoran (Author)

Caroline Corcoran is a freelance writer and editor who has previously worked at *3am Online*, *More!*, *Sugar*, *Fabulous* and *Heat*. She now writes for a variety of publications and websites on celebrity, TV, popular culture, any issues that are relevant to women and most things that people are gossiping about on Twitter. She is also writing her first novel. Follow her on Twitter @cgcorcoran

Malcolm Mackenzie (Foreword)

Malcolm Mackenzie is the editor of *We Love Pop*. He started as a professional pop fan writing for teen titles like *Top of the Pops*, *Bliss* and *TV Hits* before moving into the adult market working for *GQ*, *Glamour*, *Grazia*, *Attitude*, and newspapers such as *The Times*, *The Sunday Times*, *The Guardian* and *thelondonpaper* where he was Music Editor for three years before returning to the teen sector to launch *We Love Pop*.

Picture Credits

All images © **Getty Images**: Getty Images Entertainment: 1, 3, 23, 24, 28, 31, 38 & back cover; Getty Images for Gucci: 44; WireImage: 7, 8, 11, 12, 15, 16, 18, 21, 26, 32, front cover & 35, 41, 42, 47.